Vermont

Scenes and Seasons

Vermont
Scenes and Seasons

Photographs by George Robinson

Text by Mark Pendergrast

The New England Press
Shelburne, Vermont

Concept, text, and design © 1989 by The New England Press
Photographs © by George Robinson
All Rights Reserved
Designed by Andrea Gray

ISBN 0-933050-65-8
Library of Congress Catalog Card Number: 89-63661
Printed in China through
Four Colour Imports, Ltd., Louisville, Kentucky

For additional copies, or for a catalog of our other titles, please write:

The New England Press
P.O. Box 575
Shelburne, Vermont 05482

or e-mail: *nep@together.net*

Visit us on the web at *www.nepress.com*

Vermont
A Personal Experience

by Mark Pendergrast

• After an air-cleansing summer thunderstorm, walking on a hilltop ablaze with sudden sun. A double rainbow lighting the sky proclaims Vermont the most magical place on earth to be at this moment.

• Holding on to the gnarled bark, toes tensed, then leaping into space and falling thirty feet into a deep, cool pool in the river.

• Sitting on the deck at an elegant restaurant sipping white wine, eating unbelievable pumpkin cheesecake, listening to a classical guitarist strum quiet baroque tunes.

• Sweeping graceful curves in the virgin snow, feeling the power of the slope, in control and in sync with the world.

• Walking down a deserted dirt road at night, then lying down to look at the almost-incandescent stars. The Milky Way looks as if it has been poured across the sky.

• Screaming across Lake Champlain on a broad reach in a seventeen-foot day sailer, hiked out and glorying in the wind.

• Driving down the Interstate in autumn and almost going off the road because of the startling reds and oranges exploding on the hillsides.

• Hiking the Long Trail and meeting two couples in their seventies from Kentucky only a day away from the Canadian border. They're almost End-to-Enders.

• Stopping to buy maple syrup on a dirt road in the Northeast Kingdom and being welcomed into the home of an elderly farm couple. They say they've had one vacation in thirty years, but they wouldn't want any other way of life.

These are experiences I've had in Vermont—all just within the past year. So can you, plus many even more memorable. It is almost impossible to travel in Vermont and avoid scenes of extraordinary poignancy and beauty.

Defining Beauty

I'm not wild about "glad-word" adjectives such as *beautiful*. But what other single word could describe Vermont as well? It is full of the most startling and sometimes stark beauty, varying with the season and even with the time of day.

• The evening light dapples the ground with long shadows in the pick-your-own orchard you're harvesting, and suddenly you realize there's a beauty here entirely different from the beauty you saw when you started in the blazing afternoon sun.

• The rounded Green Mountains shade off in an undulating haze, turning bluer toward the horizon on a humid afternoon.

• You find an entire hillside carpeted with painted trillium and dainty spring beauties, nature's miracle of rebirth from beneath the snows of winter.

• Far out on an old logging trail in the middle of nowhere, you stop on your snowshoes or cross-country skis to listen to the hush of deep winter, to breathe the crispness in the air, to admire the way the snow lies fat on the branches of the spruce.

Yes, Vermont *is* beautiful, almost anywhere you turn, from historic Bennington in the south to border-hugging Derby Line in the north, from the fertile flatlands of the Champlain Valley to the rare arctic tundra atop Camel's Hump. It is the kind of landscape that turns almost anyone into a professional photographer. As you travel through the state, have your camera handy, or you'll wish you had.

To inspire you, to record just a few of the memories you'll have as you sample Vermont, we sent one of the best photographers in the state to record his favorite scenes. You'll find pictures here of a rich harvest market, of cows in no hurry crossing the road, of apple blossoms falling into a lazy river, of an old-fashioned auction, of historic sites . . . but you'll see for yourself. *Vermont: Scenes and Seasons* is a book to be savored, to be shown to friends, to be kept by the bedside to preserve the memory and beauty of what many consider America's most unusual state.

The People of Vermont

Humans can take little credit for the sort of grandeur I have described. The mountains, the streams and lakes, the changing vistas of the seasons—all are virtually the same as when the Iroquois, Abenaki, and Algonquin hunted and fished here—or, some say, the Celts, who may be responsible for the mysterious free-standing stone cellars scattered throughout the state.

As relative newcomers, though, later settlers have contributed their own brand of beauty and character to the state. Beginning with Ethan and Ira Allen and their Green Mountain Boys and continuing in an unbroken succession, Vermonters have proved themselves independent to the point of being infuriating. They are a people of dry wit, honest labor, firm opinion, and personal warmth.

You may be surprised by how talkative the supposedly taciturn Vermonters are. You may also be surprised that they take you into their homes and hearts when you express a genuine interest in their lives, their views, and their jobs. Vermonters are by and large proud of their state and eager to share that pride and knowledge.

Unspoiled Environment

One of the sources of Vermonters' pride is that, unlike many other states, Vermont has taken extra measures to assure future generations the same opportunity to appreciate its beauty and healthy living.

Back in the 1930s, for instance, the federal government proposed, as a WPA project, the Green Mountain Parkway. This scenic highway would have traversed (and ruined) the ridgeline of the mountain range. Vermonters *rejected* the idea, despite the jobs the project would have brought.

It may take you a while to notice what *isn't* here in Vermont, but when you leave, you'll surely feel assaulted by the billboards in other states. There are *no* billboards in Vermont. They were legislated out of existence long ago.

Vermont also has stiff laws controlling development. While the state is justifiably proud of having attracted major corporations such as IBM, Digital, and GE to the booming Chittenden County area, Vermont does not simply accept any new development. Laws such as Act 250 have been passed to give teeth to Vermonters' desire for reasonable growth. Several years ago, the law was put to the test when the Pyramid Company requested permission to build a mall in a suburb of Burlington. After a lengthy hearing process, Pyramid had to look elsewhere.

Geology and Geography

In the distant reaches of time, most of Vermont was a vast inland sea, which is why so many of her rocks, formed by later deformation and pressure, have a silicate base. Most of the state's mountains are the result of two tectonic plates grinding together and pushing land upward into what were once towering ranges—taller than the Rockies—about 350 million years ago.

Later, during the Ice Ages, enormous ice sheets scoured even the tallest of these peaks, grinding and rounding them, gouging new valleys, and then, as they finally melted about 12,000 years ago, depositing glacial till. Today, the average ridgeline is about 2,000 feet. A few peaks reach over 4,000 feet, including Mount Mansfield, Camel's Hump, Mount Ellen, and Mount Abraham.

It is clear from the previous sections that Vermont is a state with a backbone—both spiritually and environmentally. Its spiritual backbone is probably directly related to the *literal* backbone of mountains that runs straight up the state, somewhat to the left of the middle. The Green Mountains make up this backbone, with a smaller range, the Taconic Mountains, paralleling the Green Mountains in the south. Some of the state's most spectacular scenery and picturesque small towns are found in this central area of the state.

If you drive up scenic Route 100, you'll spend most of the time right in that backbone. You'll pass by Calvin Coolidge's homestead in Plymouth as well as the Mad River, cider mills, a priory at Weston, and the ski towns of Waitsfield and Stowe.

To the west of the Green Mountains are three distinct regions. In the south is the Vermont Valley. Here you'll find historic Bennington and the 306-foot Bennington Battle Monument, built in 1891. Although the townsfolk are proud of their spire, it is misplaced—the "Battle of Bennington" actually took place in nearby North Hoosick, New York. Here, too, you'll find untouched farming villages; Robert Todd Lincoln's estate, Hildene, with its formal gardens; and the home of Orvis fishing rods.

Farther north is the Champlain Valley, a broader expanse between Lake Champlain and the Green Mountains. Here you will find Burlington and the surrounding towns that constitute the "urban" portion of Vermont—if you can call it that. Burlington, the "Queen City" of Vermont, prides herself on her cosmopolitan flavor while retaining a small-town feeling. The pedestrian mall on Church Street in the heart of the city is a mecca for street vendors, musicians, and shoppers. In the Champlain Valley, you will also see some of the richest farmland in Vermont, as well as spectacular vistas of the Adirondacks in New York State across the lake.

Finally, in the far north, the northwest section of the state is much closer to the multicultural center of Montreal than to Boston or New York. Here you'll find the Champlain Islands, a real surprise in Vermont—they are reminiscent of Cape Cod, only much less crowded.

To the east of the Green Mountains in the south is where the first settlers discovered the potential of the state in the 1700s. In Brattleboro you'll find fine vegetarian cooking at the Common Ground Restaurant; in Vernon, the state's lone nuclear power plant; and in Newfane, a gigantic flea market and an old-fashioned country store.

Farther north is the central region, home of Montpelier, the small state capital, and Barre, her granite-quarrying sister city. Montpelier is a surprisingly accommodating city, filled with small shops, restaurants, and art galleries, and it is the home of the Vermont Historical Society.

Finally, in the rugged northern terrain carved by the teeth of the departing glaciers and full of the rocky till they left, there is the Northeast Kingdom. This unspoiled, largely undeveloped region lives up to its name. Here you will find hardworking Vermonters celebrating life on the local sledding hill or at a Saturday-night square dance much as their grandparents did. You'll also find culture: the stunning Fairbanks Museum—named after the famous scale-making family—in St. Johnsbury contains a weather station and a collection of stuffed animals, Indian artifacts, and more.

Vermont's Early History

Vermont has the distinction of being one of only a few states that were independent prior to joining the United States. It did so, reluctantly, in 1791. (Texas, much later, was also independent.) In more recent history, some have suggested that Vermont should declare its independence again, though it is *almost* certain they are joking.

White Vermonters were probably among the first permanent human settlers in the mountains. Although recent archaeological evidence suggests that various Indian tribes roamed the state more than had previously been thought, the Indians used Vermont primarily as a fishing and hunting area.

It was also a battleground between the Algonquin and the Iroquois. In July 1609, when Samuel de Champlain sailed into the lake that now bears his name, he took advantage of that animosity, siding with the Algonquin in a battle that took place on what was later the site of Fort Ticonderoga in New York.

Although the French arrived first, they failed to hold on to Vermont, despite building a fort way up north on Isle La Motte. It was the British/American colonists coming from the south who dominated its history. The British established Fort Dummer as the first permanent settlement in Vermont in 1724.

Although the French and the British had their battles—the Indians mostly sided with the French—the *real* battle of Vermont was waged among the British colonists themselves. Vermont remained a kind of no-man's-land. For some time, it was unclear whether New Hampshire, New York, or Massachusetts had a claim to it.

Enter the infamous Allen brothers. Originally from Connecticut, Ethan, Ira, Heman, and Zimri were essentially land speculators. Ethan organized a band of some two hundred followers who regularly met at Stephen Fay's Catamount Tavern in Bennington. With a gift for poetic, thundering speech, Ethan declared that "the Gods of the mountains are not the same as the Gods of the valleys" and dedicated his Green Mountain Boys to defending the title of his land claims, unceremoniously booting out Yorker land surveyors. The Yorkers called the rowdy bunch the "Bennington Mob."

The Green Mountain Boys ultimately defied the Yorkers and maneuvered Vermont into independence. The official Vermont constitution was adopted in 1777 in Windsor; the name Vermont (from *vert* and *mont*, meaning "green mountain") became official at the same time.

Ethan Allen and his Green Mountain Boys found a permanent and patriotic place in history by helping Benedict Arnold surprise the British early one morning just across Lake Champlain at Fort Ticonderoga, taking the fort without a shot being fired. Soon afterward, Allen was caught by the British. He wrote a harrowing account of his captivity, which lasted from 1775 to 1778.

Vermont after Statehood

In 1791, after the Republic of Vermont became the fourteenth state, Vermonters settled down to taming their land. The first onslaught came from making potash, their most important initial export. Potash was used in making soap and required, as its name implies, huge amounts of ash, which the settlers got from burning trees. In a way, they overdid it.

Then lumbering and sheep farming *really* laid the forests low, destroying most of the remaining trees. By 1840, virtually every Vermont farm raised sheep—there were six sheep for every person living in the state. But the opening of the Western prairies and the removal of protective tariffs killed the sheep industry. In the latter half of the eighteenth century, Vermonters turned to dairy farming, which is still the main source of farm income in the state.

Vermont retains much of its early character, remaining one of the most rural states in the country. In 1850, there were over 300,000 residents in the state. Today, there are still only about 540,000. And if you want evidence of Vermont's continued stubbornness and independence, just visit an annual town meeting in March and watch the verbal sparks fly.

Vermont's Cultural Heritage

Because Vermont is largely unspoiled and unchanged, you can see clear signs of her history and heritage almost everywhere you go. Take mills, for example. Early settlements took advantage of water power. Virtually every small town had its grist mill, saw mill, or carding mill. As industry grew, larger, more industrial mills sprang up.

Today, a few of those mills have been restored. They still saw logs or grind wheat. Mostly, however, they have been renovated as restaurants or shops. Take a moment when you're in Middlebury or Winooski to think about what life must have been like when the building you're browsing in was a functioning mill, with vast networks of whirring belts and the constant thunder of water.

Another heritage Vermont has held on to is its religious independence and fervor. At the center of every small town is a classic New England steeple. But all kinds of sects and religious communities also meet in private homes or in unusual churches constructed in a weekend of donated labor and materials.

Back in 1843, William Miller convinced many Vermonters and a good part of the United States that Judgment Day was at hand. According to Miller, the righteous, appropriately dressed in white, would be lifted off hilltops and rooftops. Unfortunately, Millerites actually perched on their roofs and simply became the laughingstocks of their neighbors.

Both Joseph Smith and Brigham Young, founders of the Mormons, were Vermonters. John Humphrey Noyes, founder of the Perfectionist sect in Putney in 1838, however, proved to be too much even for independent-minded Vermonters. He believed in sharing property in a communal setting; it turned out he also believed in sharing wives. When a local teenage girl joined his throng, her parents and the townspeople drove Noyes out of Vermont.

Another piece of Vermont history that remains alive is quarrying. Because of its geological tumult and metamorphosis, Vermont has a lot of rocks, to put it bluntly. Marble, granite, asbestos, slate, soapstone, and talc are all found in abundance here. You can see evidence of this mineral wealth all over Vermont in her fine stone buildings and elaborate tombstones.

The beautiful carving on some of those tombstones should also remind you of Vermont's ethnic heritage and diversity. Skilled artisans were imported to cut stone—from Italy, Scotland, Sweden, Hungary, and Spain. The Irish had already arrived to help build the railroads. The French-Canadians flooded over the border to work in the mills and on the farms. Today, the tradition of ethnic diversity continues as Cambodian refugees find a home in Vermont. Vermonters have always helped those oppressed by injustice—there were important stops on the Underground Railroad in the state that helped escaped slaves to reach freedom in Canada.

In a way, most of this book reflects the cultural heritage of Vermont. There is no way to cover every aspect of this unique state in such a short space, but what follows are some quick highlights of what you'll find as you roam Vermont.

Hiking

In the summer and fall, Vermont is a hiker's paradise. The Long Trail, conceived in 1909 and finished in 1931, extends some 263 miles from the Massachusetts border to Canada. In addition, there are about a hundred side trails, so the whole Long Trail system covers a total of about 440 miles.

Before tackling the Long Trail (or earning your End-to-Ender badge), you should be aware that it is *not* easy hiking. Sure, there are some milder stretches; but by and large the trail goes out of its way to hit every peak, and it isn't always genteel in how it does it. In other words, be prepared for stretches of extremely steep, muddy, rocky trail.

It's worth it, though, once you've reached one of the sturdy shelters or arrived atop a peak with a 360-degree view of Vermont. Take a day and hike to the top of my favorite high peak, Camel's Hump. You can pick up the pocket-size *Guide Book of the Long Trail* in any Vermont bookstore.

For the less ambitious hiker, there are innumerable gentler trails in Vermont. Try little Mount Philo in Ferrisburg or the Pinnacle in Stowe if you want to feel you've reached the top but don't want to take all day doing it. The Green Mountain Club puts out another easy-to-carry book, the *Day Hiker's Guide to Vermont*, which will head you in the right direction. Even a short nature walk without a steep climb will introduce you to the beauties of Vermont's forests, wildlife, and streams.

As I've pointed out, Vermont was once "logged over." Few trees from the time of the Revolutionary War are still standing. Vermont is a state in which you can see nature taking over from man rather than the other way around. In fact, entire abandoned communities are scattered throughout the Vermont hills. As you hike along, you may suddenly realize you're walking on an old road, not just on a hiking trail, and that stone wall running through the woods was probably for cows. If you look closely, you might see a cellar hole. Dig around a bit, and you'll become an amateur archaeologist, unearthing the beautiful blue bottles that once held Lydia Pinkham's potions.

Of Trees, Flowers, and Gardens

The trees of the state are spectacular—particularly in the fall, of course. Sugar maple and beech dominate the lower slopes of the mountains. Higher up, you'll find yellow and white birch and red spruce. If you continue up a mountain, spruce and balsam fir dominate; then they get smaller and smaller, and you're above the treeline altogether.

As you walk or drive, see if you can spot the different stands of trees. There's something magical about a delicate grouping of luminous white birch, for instance. It's also called paper birch—the Indians used the easily peeled bark for canoes and writing.

Of course, the *most* magical Vermont tree is the sugar maple. These large, gnarled, dignified trees yield to the tap every spring when the days are warm but the nights still have a snap to them. The sap flows into buckets, the buckets are dumped into evaporating pans with fires beneath them, and at the right moment—aaah!—maple syrup. Visit a sugar house in the spring for that ambrosial mist coming from the pans and for freshly boiled syrup on snow ("sugar-on-snow").

Then come back in the fall and see the same trees provide a color show unequaled anywhere else in nature. Painters have tried to match the exact shades of orange and red, but they can't touch the real thing.

The wildflowers of Vermont, growing in the pastures or in the under-story of the forests, are also worth studying or simply admiring. In 1935, Vermont's late Senator George Aiken wrote a classic little book, *Pioneering with Wildflowers*, that is still accurate and highly readable. Even the names of the flowers are beautiful and expressive: saxifrage, trillium, spring beauty, showy ladyslipper, bloodroot, foamflower, goldthread, shooting star, walking leaf fern, creeping snowberry.

Finally, stop in a small Vermont town—or a large one, for that matter—and admire a garden. The hardest-hearted homesteader will melt when he or she realizes you've stopped to ask just *how* anyone could grow pumpkins that large or an asparagus patch that lush. Vermonters take great pride in their gardens and grow an astonishing variety of food in a short season. You'll find watermelon and okra as well as corn, beans, peas, and lettuce. Chances are, the happy gardener will force produce on you until you can't hold any more.

Vermont Animals and Wildlife

Vermonters love their animals, even when they never see them. The last known Vermont catamount (also known as a panther) was shot in 1881 and is still fierce—though stuffed—in the Vermont Historical Society Museum in Montpelier. Nonetheless, some say catamounts, shy creatures, are still stalking the Vermont woods.

I can personally testify that there are bears in Vermont. I tried to raise bees last year, but a bear decided just before winter arrived that he would have a final delicacy: my bees' honey.

I never saw the bear, but I *have* seen fox, skunk, porcupines, beaver, mice, and deer. I even had a little Bambi visit me in my garden while her nervous mother hovered in the trees. The occasional moose still wanders out of the woods as well, including the now-famous Bullwinkle, who fell in love with Jessica the cow. The wild turkey has successfully been re-introduced. Fish ladders around dams are allowing Atlantic salmon to spawn once again in Vermont waters.

Don't forget to look for the smaller Vermont animals. A friendly chipmunk or deer mouse will capture your heart—and some of your trail mix too—near one of the hiking shelters.

Vermonters raise almost every type of animal imaginable. Besides cows, sheep are making a strong comeback for both wool and meat. Pigs, llamas, goats, chickens, guinea hens, ducks, geese, rabbits, turkeys, and who knows what else—you'll find them all on Vermont farms.

Inns and Restaurants

Vermont has a phenomenal number of good places to eat. First, there are the country inns. These range from simple, wholesome bed-and-breakfasts to two-hundred-year-old mansions serving gourmet meals. Each has its own character and history. So even if you don't stay at the inns—and you should—at least stop for a meal and a chat.

And if you like to combine adventure, comfort, and sumptuous dining, you might try one of Vermont's inn-to-inn biking or hiking tours.

Vermont restaurants offer some of the finest cooking available anywhere, ranging from old-fashioned country cooking to traditional Italian, French, and Oriental cuisine. Because of Vermont's beauty and reputation, many European chefs have found their way here. They have been joined by chefs trained at Montpelier's Culinary Institute of Vermont.

Cemeteries

Though this may sound gruesome to you, cemeteries are some of the most interesting, relaxing places in Vermont. Take a picnic to a graveyard if you're in a quiet, contemplative mood. There are cemeteries great and small all over Vermont; chances are, you'll be fascinated by an instant history lesson and charmed by the peaceful surroundings.

I visited a Burlington cemetery recently, the one off Colchester Avenue with a monument to Ethan Allen, whose elusive remains are supposedly buried somewhere nearby. The lichen-covered stones yield names with character: Ichabod Brownell; Sabra, wife of Henry Boardman; Freelove, daughter of Amos and Polly Wilkins; Zebina, son of Absalom and Sally Packard.

You'll find a lot of sons and daughters. In the 1800s in Vermont, death hovered near children. Epidemics of "spotted fever" (cerebrospinal meningitis) wiped out whole families. Women died in childbirth. The Zebina mentioned above was seven months old when he died on July 9, 1802. The Fobes family lost Luther in 1801, aged sixteen months. He drowned, according to the stone. Next to him lies his sister Rachel, who died in 1806 at seventeen months.

Finally, there is the following poignant and tantalizing gravestone: "In memory of Ruthy Morgan, consort of Bela Morgan, who died March 1, 1814, age 20 years, her infant babe at her side."

Water, Water Sports, and Fishing

Minnesota may be the "land of lakes," but Vermont could be the "land of ponds and streams." Of course, it has magnificent lakes as well. Lake Champlain, the largest freshwater lake in the United States besides the Great Lakes, is only fourteen miles wide at its broadest point but is a hundred miles long. As part of the Inland Waterway, it has long served as a commercial route. Nowadays, it is loaded with recreational boats. During the many sailboat races, when the fleet is headed downwind, the lake is decorated with colorful spinnakers bellying in the wind.

Take one of the ferry trips, or board the *Homer Dixon*, Lake Champlain's windjammer charter, offering three- to six-day cruises. Or don scuba gear and find one of the historic wrecks lying at the bottom of Lake Champlain. Half of the other really large lake in Vermont rests in Canada. Lake Memphremagog, like Lake Champlain, offers fine fishing and boating.

Vermont is famous for her trout streams and ponds. Just looking at the state map is tantalizing. Each pond or stream has its own local lore and secret fishing holes. Asking how a pond got its name can be a good way to start a local conversation. There's Horse Pond, Caspian Lake, May Pond, Joe's Pond, Echo Lake, Gale Meadows Pond, Grout Pond, Lake Raponda, Lake Rescue, Crystal Lake, Arrowhead Mountain Lake, Weatherhead Hollow Pond, and Ticklenaked Pond. Not to mention Stickney Brook, Rake Brook, Lemon Fair River, and Minister Brook.

Canoeing in Vermont can be either an exciting whitewater experience or a calm drift. You can try the huge Connecticut River on the eastern border or the west-flowing Winooski and Lamoille rivers. Or paddle quietly by tiny summer camps on one of the ponds or lakes.

In the summer, ask about the best local swimming hole. While swimming in lakes and ponds is enjoyable, it is often more exciting to find a place where a bracing brook has carved a pool into the rock—and if you're brave or crazy, you can often find a safe place to jump into that pool. Even if you don't want to swim there, these pools and gorges offer breathtaking scenery and are often only a short walk from the road.

Skiing and Winter Sports

Vermont offers the best downhill skiing in the eastern United States. Stowe is probably the most famous ski area, with beautifully groomed trails on Mount Mansfield, Vermont's highest mountain. There are numerous other major areas such as Killington, Bolton, Suicide Six, Jay Peak, Sugarbush, Haystack, and Okemo.

Although these larger areas undoubtedly offer more reliable and exciting skiing, I must admit to a prejudice in favor of the smaller, lesser-known hills, where you don't have to fight lift lines and where you meet more locals.

Vermont was the site of the first ski tow in the United States—on Gilbert's Hill in Woodstock in 1933. It was operated by an old tractor engine. You can still find an almost identical setup at Northeast Slopes in East Corinth. Begun in 1936 as a neighborhood slope, it has never grown. Today it is powered by a 1960 Ford farm truck. Other smaller slopes include Cochran's in Richmond and Lyndon Outing Club in Lyndonville. Two colleges also provide excellent, quiet downhill facilities: Norwich University in Northfield and the Middlebury Snow Bowl in Ripton.

If you *really* want quiet and exercise, try cross-country skiing. It's inexpensive, healthy, and offers breathtaking solitary vistas. There are numerous well-groomed trails in Vermont; the most famous is the Trapp Family Lodge in Stowe. At Trapp's, you can work your way up and up and up to a cabin with hot chocolate, homemade soup, and a roaring fire before blasting down in a well-earned downhill spurt.

Besides the for-pay cross-country areas, you might try the free snowmobile trails. Just be ready to get off the trail when you hear that characteristic buzzing in the distance that announces the approach of a Ski-Doo.

You might even join the snowmobilers yourself. It's an exciting—if noisy—way to see Vermont's woods in the winter. Or don snowshoes and don't be fettered by trails at all. Better bring a compass or a native along, though.

Finally, don't forget all those ponds and lakes we talked about. They're frozen now, so solidly that many folks drive their cars right out onto Lake Champlain to their favorite ice-fishing spot. An ice auger drills a neat hole, and the perch are hungrier and easier to catch in the winter. You can also join the fanatical iceboaters as they skim across the lake at speeds of sixty miles per hour or better.

Camping and State Parks

Although you *may* want to go camping in the winter—and more people are wild about winter camping than you'd believe—you'll probably want to restrict this activity to the warmer months. You can always backpack with a tent. But if you prefer car-camping, I recommend Vermont's well-maintained state park, almost all of which are on or near water; most host nature programs and feature clean sites.

Having said that, I urge you to leave your car anyway and try Burton Island State Park, near St. Albans. This intimate island can be reached only by boat. No cars are allowed, and you'll be glad. There are comfortable shelters for camping and quiet trails, and it's a birder's paradise.

Other favorite state parks are near Groton (New Discovery, Big Deer, Boulder Beach, and Ricker). Half Moon Pond State Park, near Hubbardton, is a gem next to a tiny pond.

Theater and Music

For such a rural state, Vermont offers a plethora of cultural activities, particularly in theater and music. Even the smaller towns often have an "opera house," where you can find lively summer musicals. Try the Weston Playhouse or the offerings of the Lamoille County Players in the Hyde Park Opera House, for instance. Check the local papers wherever you happen to be traveling.

Colleges also offer excellent theater, both during the academic year and in the summer. The University of Vermont offers the Champlain Shakespeare Festival at the Royall Tyler Theater in Burlington. Here you will see inventive professional stagings of plays by the Bard as well as other playwrights. St. Michael's College offers professional summer theater in nearby Winooski.

The hills of Vermont are indeed alive with the sound of music, and not just in Stowe, where the Trapp Family settled. Offerings range from the Craftsbury Chamber Players and the Marlboro Music Festival to bluegrass and fiddle contests. The Vermont Mozart Festival concerts are often held outdoors on the green sweep of the Shelburne Farms lawns. Here, cows listen placidly to the strains of baroque favorites.

Vermont Food Specialties

Everywhere you go in Vermont, Vermonters will offer you delicious homemade fare, and I'm not just talking about maple syrup. You'd be foolish not to spend some of your traveling money on souvenirs that you can enjoy devouring once you're home.

Take chocolates, for instance. Champlain Chocolates makes truffles that are no trifles. These little goodies rival the best European delicacies. Or try Vermont's own Champ's Chips, all-natural potato chips with a crunch that will send you back for more. They're named for Champ, the Lake Champlain monster who rivals Nessie in her elusive appearances.

If you like jellies, jams, or dressings, especially with a maple or mustard flavor, Vermont is the place to be. Fresh fruit is also abundant. In season, seek out one of Vermont's many apple or pear orchards, where you can pick your own perfect specimens of Mac, Empire, Golden Delicious, or Northern Spy. Other "pick your own" operations are ubiquitous, too. Strawberries, fat, red, and juicy. Raspberries, blueberries. Right off the plant and into your mouth.

Try the distillation of some of the apples in one of Vermont's cider mills. There you can watch the presses squeeze that golden liquid just for you. Another delicious by-product of the orchards is honey. Vermont apiaries offer the bees' sweet product in crystalline or comb honey, in addition to the regular golden flow. The taste varies, depending on the blossoms the bees dined on.

You like cheese? There are cheese producers across the state, turning Vermont cows' milk into everything from brie to sharp cheddar. You've probably already discovered another transmutation of Vermont milk, but if you haven't, buy some Ben & Jerry's ice cream. I'm partial to White Russian, but others swear by Heathbar Crunch. You can get samples during a tour of the Ben & Jerry's plant in Waterbury Center.

One of Ethan Allen's cousins was named Remember Baker. I doubt he spent much time in the kitchen, but his name reminds me that Vermont bakers are among the best in the country. From pumpernickel to whole wheat to sourdough, they'll keep you coming back for more. They've even mastered the bagel, rivaling New York City varieties in chewable flavor.

In the early days of Vermont, every town had its own brewery or winery. In recent years, fine brews have returned to the state. You can sample full-bodied Catamount Beer, made in White River Junction, or hard cider and wine from the Cerniglia Winery in Cavendish.

Museums and Art Galleries

Vermont offers a variety of museums and art galleries. One place you can't pass up is the Shelburne Museum, which offers a forty-five acre tour back in time. Here you can see the now-landlocked steamboat *Ticonderoga*, as well as weaving demonstrations, a huge Victorian doll collection, and a miniature circus.

But there are also exquisite smaller finds such as the Fleming Museum in Burlington, the Mary Bryan Art Gallery in Jeffersonville, the New England Maple Museum in Pittsford, or the American Precision Museum and Vermont State Craft Center in Windsor. Almost every town has a historical society worth checking out. In addition, craft stores offer browsing as well as viewing opportunities. Frog Hollow Craft Center in Middlebury is one of the largest of its kind.

Educational Innovations, Bookstores, and Libraries

Maybe it's because the long winters encourage reading. But whatever the reason, Vermonters are an exceptionally well-read, educated lot. One of my former neighbors, an eighty-year-old blacksmith and berrygrower, never finished the eighth grade—but he has memorized the Bible and an encyclopedia.

Some of the most innovative educational institutions and programs in the country began in Vermont. Goddard College in Plainfield was an early avant-garde institution in Vermont. Students at the Putney School, founded in 1935, combine studies with farm chores. Both Middlebury College and the Experiment in International Living in Brattleboro specialize in multilingual and cross-cultural studies. The University of Vermont in Burlington is one of the finest research institutions in the United States.

You might consider taking advantage of course offerings. Contact some of the schools to see if they offer special summer residence programs. But you don't have to enroll to enjoy books in Vermont. There are plenty of bookstores. My favorites are the used bookstores, where you never know what treasures you'll find—or at what bargain price.

Even better bargains are the local Vermont libraries. They're free and are often an excellent place (along with the town clerk's office) to ask questions about local events. Andrew Carnegie funded many of the gemlike small-town Vermont libraries. Although they are not always open as many hours as you might like, they offer surprisingly efficient service through a newly computerized statewide interlibrary-loan system.

Classic Vermont Villages

Here is a recipe for enjoying a real Vermont village in any season. Get a free *Vermont Official State Map and Touring Guide* from a filling station or tourist stop. Or if you really want to do it right, buy one of the larger Vermont road atlases now available. These show every dirt road in the state.

Now, find a back road. It shouldn't be too hard. Even if you're in the Big City of Burlington, it won't take more than a half hour. Drive slowly, and look. Look for the signs of whatever season it is on the farms you pass.

The fields may lie fallow under snow—one of the best fertilizers nature has to offer, by the way. Get out if you want and look for animal tracks. Watch the way the smoke from the wood fires goes straight up into the cold air. Smell that smoke, the promise of warmth inside.

Perhaps it's spring, and the birds are just coming back. The redwing blackbirds sit on every other fencepost singing their hearts out to establish their territory—or just for the joy of it. A tractor makes the neat rounds of a field, plowing the rich soil for another season.

Perhaps it's high summer, and the corn is greening up to shoulder height and all of nature is at a fever pitch to produce, knowing how short a time it has.

Maybe it's autumn. The bound hay lies in huge rounded bales, like giant loaves of shredded wheat. The pungent smell of Vermont's country perfume lets you know a manure spreader is nearby. The leaves are beginning to turn. That bittersweet feeling of fall is in the air.

Keep driving. Slowly. Eventually you'll come to a small town. Find the village green. There are so many classic greens to choose from in Vermont. They are in the center of town, a visible symbol of commitment to conservative values, care of the land, and small-town life.

Have a seat on one of the benches, and just watch life go by for a while. Listen to the birds. Then take a walk through the town. You have no object in mind. Admire the architecture. It might be Greek or Gothic Revival, Federalist, Second Empire, or Queen Anne. Or you might just call it country revival.

Find a general store. There really are still such institutions in Vermont. They sell penny candy, jumper cables, corncob pipes, and custom-butchered meats. Browse around. Buy something you don't really need.

Find the bridge crossing the inevitable stream or river. Maybe it's one of Vermont's many covered bridges. Maybe it's a one-lane affair; drivers know they have to wait their turn. Stand on the bridge and watch the river slipping slowly away.

Find the local diner. If you're lucky, you'll find an authentic former dining car, and you can order an old-fashioned open-faced turkey sandwich, with plenty of gravy and bona fide mashed potatoes.

Does a railroad run through town? Maybe the old station has been converted to a restaurant or store. Maybe a special foliage train excursion is available.

There might be an auction going on for the local Rotary. Hang out in back and marvel at the speedy nonsense that tumbles hypnotically from the auctioneer's mouth. Buy a grab-bag for two dollars. Or find a local flea market or garage sale or antique shop. (If it's a small enough town, you can safely call it a junk shop while you buy the antiques.)

You might luck out and come to town during the local field days. There might be a horse or ox-pulling contest, a wood-splitting event, or a pie-eating contest. There are sure to be some booths and games, a miniature version of the midway at the Champlain Valley Fair held each summer in Essex Junction.

From anywhere, find the church spire. Seek out a contemplative moment inside. Look at the church bulletin board to see if there's a dime-a-dip church supper available.

Wander back to the green. Find your bench. Think about where you want to go tomorrow. Or don't think at all.

Until Next Time . . .

Now that you've visited Vermont, you'll understand why my blacksmith neighbor (the one who memorized the encyclopedia) made the following prediction to a young man bound for warmer climes: "You'll be back. People who've lived in Vermont always come back."

I was that young man. May the same prediction also hold true for you.

First Congregational Church, Bennington

West Brookfield

Pleasant Valley (*opposite*)

Sap Buckets

Country Lane

Huntington (*overleaf*)

School Day

Goat with Woodpile

The Capitol, Montpelier

Emptying the Sap Buckets

Randolph

Jericho

The Champlain Valley Fair, Essex Junction

Cambridge

Mount Mansfield (*overleaf*)

Hauling Wood

Full Moon (*opposite*)

The Bennington Battle Monument

Cattle Crossing

Town Meeting, Panton

Town Meeting, Panton

Irish Settlement Road, Underhill

Covered Bridge in the Mist

West Brookfield (*overleaf*)

Waits River

The Florence V. Cilley General Store, Plymouth

Stowe

Jericho

Getting the Mail

Lake Champlain (*opposite*)

Underhill

Harvest Market

Windsurfing on Lake Champlain (*overleaf*)

Boyhood Home of Calvin Coolidge, Plymouth

Norwich (*opposite*)

Ice-Fishing Shanties, Malletts Bay

Apple Blossoms (*opposite*)

Ethan Allen Monument, Burlington

Playing in the Leaves

The Auction Barn

Camel's Hump

Underhill (*overleaf*)

West Woodstock

Strafford

The Round Church, Richmond

Mount Mansfield

Essex

Killington (*opposite*)

Ira Allen Chapel, Burlington

Plainfield

Lake Champlain (*overleaf*)